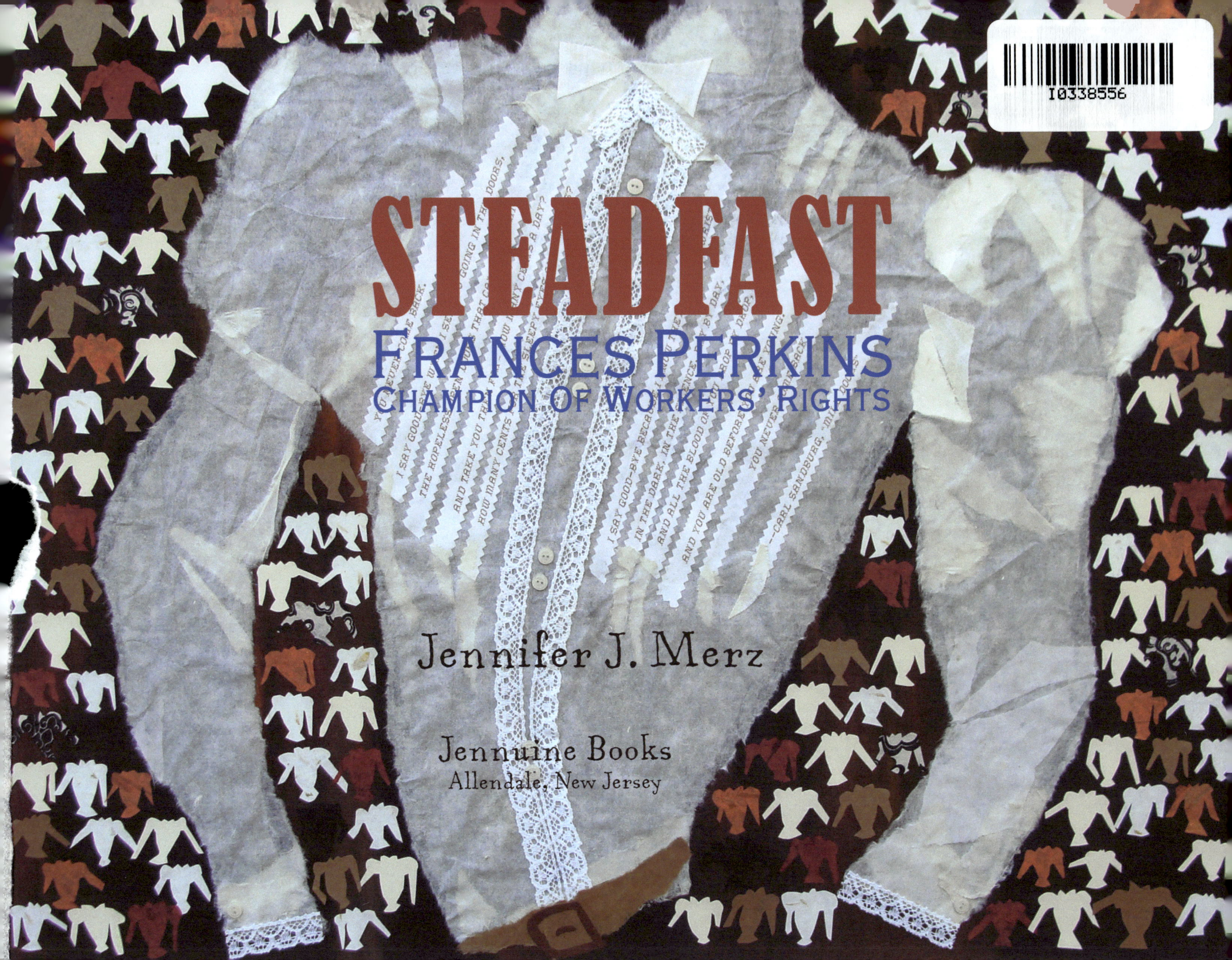

STEADFAST
FRANCES PERKINS
CHAMPION OF WORKERS' RIGHTS

Jennifer J. Merz

Jennuine Books
Allendale, New Jersey

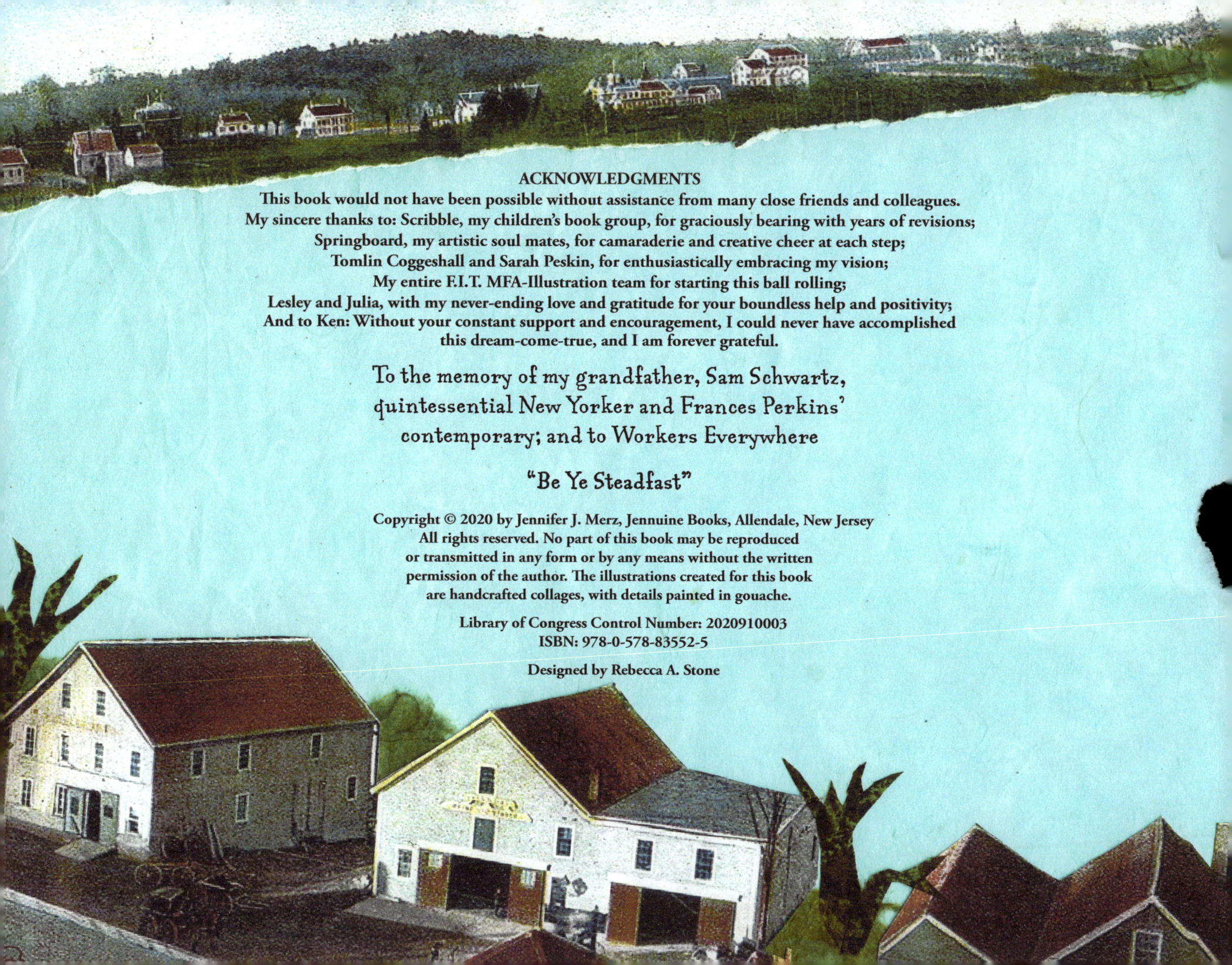

ACKNOWLEDGMENTS

This book would not have been possible without assistance from many close friends and colleagues.
My sincere thanks to: Scribble, my children's book group, for graciously bearing with years of revisions;
Springboard, my artistic soul mates, for camaraderie and creative cheer at each step;
Tomlin Coggeshall and Sarah Peskin, for enthusiastically embracing my vision;
My entire F.I.T. MFA-Illustration team for starting this ball rolling;
Lesley and Julia, with my never-ending love and gratitude for your boundless help and positivity;
And to Ken: Without your constant support and encouragement, I could never have accomplished this dream-come-true, and I am forever grateful.

To the memory of my grandfather, Sam Schwartz, quintessential New Yorker and Frances Perkins' contemporary; and to Workers Everywhere

"Be Ye Steadfast"

Copyright © 2020 by Jennifer J. Merz, Jennuine Books, Allendale, New Jersey
All rights reserved. No part of this book may be reproduced or transmitted in any form or by any means without the written permission of the author. The illustrations created for this book are handcrafted collages, with details painted in gouache.

Library of Congress Control Number: 2020910003
ISBN: 978-0-578-83552-5

Designed by Rebecca A. Stone

Heroes come in all shapes and sizes, but this one had sparkling brown eyes, a calm voice, caring spirit, and most of all, steadfast determination. She was born Fannie Coralie Perkins to a loving but stern New England family in 1880.

"Think about what you want to say before you say it," Father said. Unlike most dads in those days, he believed that girls should be educated and that women should be allowed to vote. Mother encouraged Fannie to help others. She gave her daughter a simple, sturdy hat and said, "There you are, dear. Just like you: plain and dependable."

Fannie spent carefree summers surrounded by the fragrant gardens of her grandparents' farm in Maine. There, Granny's homestead was as warm as fresh-baked pie. Granny would often say, "Fannie, when a door opens, you must always walk through."

When the door to college opened, Fannie eagerly bounded through. Her classmates called her Perk; she was filled with bright ideas and liked to get things done. *Be Ye Steadfast* was the class motto. It fit Fannie's dedicated personality perfectly.

"I discovered for the first time...that I had a mind."

One day, Fannie had a class trip to a factory. Machines clanked in dreary rooms caked with grime and dust. Fannie coughed. She blinked. She shook her head. *Children at work? Adults at dangerous jobs?* She decided right then to become a social worker. Soon out of college, she officially changed her name to Frances and began looking for a job to assist needy families.

"I had to do something about…unnecessary poverty. It was sort of up to me."

Before long, Frances worked in New York City, inspecting factories for their safety. The city buzzed and hummed to the beat of a new era. Each day, throngs of immigrants sailed into port on bellowing steamships. Most arrived with hopeful hearts but empty pockets and growling stomachs.

And how they suffered. They labored long hours for too-little pay at backbreaking jobs in filthy factories. They endured bleak nights in cold, cramped tenements. Frances' heart ached. No matter how hard the immigrants worked, they had no way to get ahead.

"Why don't you get married?" asked her mother.
"Why don't you teach school?" asked her father.
"Maybe you should push through a new door," said Granny.
Frances gave Granny a hug. That sounded just right.

Frances began to press for new ways of thinking. She marched for women's rights and fought for a shorter workweek. She joined others to organize unions and change laws. She imagined a world without child labor. She dreamed of fairness and safety for all workers, no matter where they came from, no matter what their backgrounds.

Frances had heard of the Triangle Waist Company, a large factory perched on the top three stories of New York City's Asch Building. There, from dawn to dusk, hundreds of immigrant girls and young women hunched over sewing machines making shirtwaists, the fashionable women's blouse with buttons down the front, a cinched-in waist, and big puffy sleeves.

Girls and young women sat jam-packed in deafening clatter, fingers flying over collars and cuffs. Machines spit, sparked, and sputtered like angry hornets. "Hurry up!" greedy bosses boomed.

Dim, dusty rooms overflowed with flimsy fabrics. Paper patterns dangled above. Bins brimmed with remnants. Baskets blocked aisles. Exit doors were locked and girls routinely searched to prevent theft.

If workers were sick or hurt, they were fired. If they pricked their fingers and bled on the cloth, they paid for the damages. If they were late, they lost half a day's pay. Late again, they were let go. The girls paid for electricity, paid for thread, paid for the chairs they sat on.

This is not the America of dreams! fumed Frances.

Then, at closing time on the bright spring afternoon of Saturday, March 25, 1911, catastrophe struck.

Frances was having tea with friends when fire trucks thundered past the window. She jumped from her seat, dashed outside, and peered up the street.

The Triangle Factory was ablaze!

Flames swiftly spread.
Rising heat shattered glass.
Black smoke billowed.
Flames shot out the window.
Smoke and fear were everywhere.

Bells clanged, sirens howled, whistles shrieked, workers screamed.

Fire!

Frances rushed to the gathering crowd, heart pounding. A sooty, smoky smell filled her nostrils. She looked up and saw a horrible sight.

In the factory, workers scrambled. They hoisted their long skirts, raced down narrow hallways and yanked on locked doors.

They tried the rickety fire escape, but it crashed down.

They leaped into the elevator, but its cable snapped.

The fire department came quickly, but the ladders were too short.

Some workers clamored to the roof and escaped. They thanked heaven and wept with relief.

From the street, Frances could make out girls teetering on window ledges. "Don't jump!" yelled the crowd. In desperation, girls jumped but *alas!* Firemen's nets couldn't save them.

"It was a horrifying spectacle."

The fire was out. The sky sobbed. New York City gasped and wailed,

If only the doors weren't locked.
If only the fire escape were stronger.
If only ladders were longer.
If only . . ., if only . . ., if only . . . !

But Frances didn't say *if only*. Deep inside, she felt the fury of a different kind of flame. Life had a purpose for Frances—and she was ready to embrace it. She dried her tears, grit her teeth, and said, "Next time."

Next time, factory doors will not be locked.
Next time, fire escapes will be strong.
Next time, workers will get out safely.
Our dear sisters did not die in vain!

"I felt I must sear it not only on my mind but on my heart as a never-to-be-forgotten reminder of why I had to spend my life fighting conditions that could permit such a tragedy."

The Women's Trade Union League held a public meeting. The hall roared with determination. Anger and despair turned to steely resolve. Change was in the air.

Frances became a fire prevention expert and spoke throughout the city. "Workplaces must be made safe," she insisted.

New York State created a Factory Investigating Commission with Frances as chief investigator. She inspected buildings to make sure business owners cooperated with new rules. She bargained with dishonest politicians if she had to. Anything to avoid another tragedy.

Just three years after the fire, thirty-three new labor laws existed. "A turning point!" pronounced Frances.

Frances' male colleagues grumbled, "We won't work with a woman!" Some threatened to quit. Frances had to figure out how be taken seriously in government rooms filled with men. She noticed that the men respected their mothers, so she dressed in a matronly style: black dress, pearls, prim and proper black hat. *This is how I can get things done.* It worked. They listened to the calm voice and bright ideas of the trailblazer in their midst.

"Being a woman has only bothered me in climbing trees."

Soon, President Franklin Delano Roosevelt needed someone he could count on to fight for workers' rights. He asked Frances to be the Secretary of Labor, the first woman in a U.S. Presidential Cabinet. But Frances wouldn't walk through that door unless he considered the big, bold plan in her pocket.

She nervously took out the crinkled paper and read it out loud to the newly-elected president. Her plan would protect workers throughout the nation. It would change the role of government. Nothing like this had ever been attempted in the United States before.

"The door might not be opened to a woman again for a long, long time..."

"Can I do it?" she asked.

"Yes, yes, yes, you can do it," said the president with the wave of his hand. He knew how determined Frances could be.

Her plan became the foundation of the New Deal, programs that championed all American workers: *No more child labor. A forty-hour workweek. A guaranteed minimum wage. Help for unemployed or injured workers.* Frances gave a deep, satisfied sigh. Her dreams of fairness and safety in the workplace were coming true.

Frances didn't stop there. She pictured Granny and knew that many older people struggled to pay their bills. Frances studied long and hard and came up with a dazzling new idea. The president signed it into law and Frances swelled with pride as the Mother of Social Security.

"I promise to use what brains I have to meet problems with intelligence and courage."

35

Frances visited Granny's homestead often. She breathed in the sweet, clear, country air. It was the perfect place to stop and listen for answers to complex problems.

When Frances married and had a daughter, she continued going to work and kept her maiden name for her career. "Shocking!" people said, but Frances shrugged. She was too busy defending workers' rights to pay attention.

"I have discovered the rule of silence is one of the most beautiful things in the world."

Frances was always a friend to the working person. Her legacy continues—all because the perky problem solver from Maine had the courage to dry her tears, summon her strength, stay steadfast to her goals, and walk through open doors.

"The people are what matter to government, and a government should aim to give all [its] people... the best possible life."

Photo Courtesy of the Frances Perkins Center

"There is always a large horizon ... There is much to be done ...
I am not going to be doing it! It is up to you."

SAFETY REFORMS

Many current safety rules exist thanks to reforms championed by Frances Perkins following the Triangle Factory Fire:

- Exits unlocked throughout business hours
- Exit doors swing out
- Exit signs posted in clear, red letters
- Occupancy limitations posted
- Suitable lighting and ventilation
- Automatic shut-offs on dangerous machinery
- Multiple fire exits
- Clear paths to exits
- Fire extinguishers on site
- Working fire escapes
- Automatic sprinkler systems for seventh story and up
- Mandatory, regular fire drills
- Emergency evacuation plans posted
- Regular maintenance of hazardous materials
- Workplace trash bins emptied nightly
- Smoking in factories prohibited
- Factories registered for regular safety checks
- Clean drinking water and sanitary, ventilated restrooms
- Children required to obtain a doctor's note for employment, confirming that they are fourteen-years-old or older

THE NEW DEAL

Frances Perkins was the driving force behind the New Deal, the vast series of government programs signed into law by President Franklin D. Roosevelt. It helped countless workers survive the hardships of the Great Depression. Frances' list of tasks to be worked on by the newly-elected president looked like this:

- A forty-hour workweek
- A minimum wage
- Abolishment of child labor
- Unemployment insurance
- Workman's compensation
- Social Security (as part of the Social Security Act of 1935)
- Health insurance for all citizens
  (this objective was not met, and is still unachieved today)

FRANCES PERKINS: CHRONOLOGY OF A LONG AND PRODUCTIVE LIFE

1880	Fannie Coralie Perkins born April 10th, in Boston; childhood summers in Newcastle, ME with grandparents
1898	Graduates Worcester Classical High School, Worcester, MA
1902	Graduates Mount Holyoke College, South Hadley, MA
1904	Teaches in Lake Forest, IL and volunteers at Hull House, Chicago, IL
1905	Changes name to Frances Perkins
1907	Graduate study Wharton School of the University of Pennsylvania
1909	Moves to New York with a fellowship to Columbia University; speaks on soap boxes and at rallies for women's suffrage
1910	Master's degree from Columbia University; hired by New York Consumers' League to inspect factories; works to abolish child labor, and lobbies for 'shorter' 54-hour workweek
1911	Eyewitnesses Triangle Factory Fire, March 25th, New York City
1912-15	Hired by Committee on Safety of the City of New York, citizens' group created in response to fire; expert witness and primary investigator for state Factory Investigating Commission leading to first workplace health and safety laws in nation
1913	Marries Paul C. Wilson, September 26th
1916	Daughter Susanna born, December 30th
1918	First Executive Secretary of Maternity Center Association
1919	First woman on New York State Industrial Commission
1921	Executive secretary of the Council on Immigrant Education
1922	A commissioner of the NYS Industrial Board; becomes chairman 1926
1929	New York State Industrial Commissioner
1933	U.S. Secretary of Labor, first woman in U.S. Cabinet
1933-45	Major accomplishments as Secretary of Labor include: Social Security Act: landmark law establishing old age pensions, unemployment insurance, survivor benefits CCC, NRA, PWA, WPA: Instrumental in New Deal jobs programs U.S. Employment Service: Created by Wagner-Peyser Act Fair Labor Standards Act: Max hours and min wages; restrictions on child labor, Bureau of Labor Standards: Industrial accident and occupational disease prevention; working condition improvements through research and union/employers conferences National Labor Relations Act: Right of workers to organize, collective bargaining International Labor Org: Coordinated effort for U.S. membership Immigration: Saved thousands of refugees by limiting deportations to Nazi Germany
1945-53	Appointed to U.S. Civil Service Commission
1946	Writes best-selling biography of FDR titled "The Roosevelt I Knew"
1957-65	Visiting professor: Cornell University's ILR School
1965	Dies May 14th, New York, NY

❧ AFTERWORD ❧

At the beginning of the twentieth century, over five thousand immigrants came to America daily, arriving through Ellis Island, NY. Most were from Russia, Italy, and Eastern Europe, looking to escape religious persecution and financial hardship. Their hopes of a better life were dashed when they found themselves trapped in abject poverty.

The immigrants lived in dingy, airless tenements that were freezing in winter and sweltering in summer. As many as 2,500 people lived in one city block. Buildings had one toilet for twenty people and no place to bathe. Children worked in factories or sweatshops up to twelve hours a day, six days a week. There were no laws to protect minors; school was a luxury. Workers seldom quit out of desperate need.

These were the wretched circumstances that youthful, compassionate Frances Perkins discovered as she investigated labor conditions for the National Consumers' League of New York City. These conditions were the backdrop to the tragic Triangle Factory Fire. Of the one-hundred-and-forty-six people who perished in the fire on March 25, 1911, most were girls or young women, ages thirteen to twenty-three, Jewish or Italian immigrants.

The Triangle Fire set the wheels in motion for radical workplace reform. Before the fire, the government assumed it had no power to regulate business. As attitudes shifted, laws were passed to protect the American worker. Frances was there, doggedly pressing for improvements every step of the way.

Frances was a bold advocate for the American laborer. Her courageous achievements culminated in her accomplishments as Franklin Delano Roosevelt's Secretary of Labor. As the first woman in a Presidential Cabinet, she was the force behind the New Deal, the sweeping social programs signed into law by FDR during the Great Depression of the 1930s. Frances would later say that the New Deal was born on March 25, 1911, at the Triangle.

❧ NOTES ❧

Frances Perkins inherited the Perkins' homestead in Newcastle, Maine in 1927. Built as a wedding present for her grandmother, it was kept in the Perkins family until 2020 when it became home to the Frances Perkins Center, an educational organization dedicated to preserving and sharing her legacy. Please visit www.FrancesPerkinsCenter.org to learn more.

Jennifer Merz divides her time between the NY-Metro area and the Maine coast. She and her husband are proud parents of two spirited women who, like Frances, walk assuredly through open doors. Go to www.jennifermerz.com for more.

❧ AUTHOR'S NOTE ❧

I could never have imagined that my participation in an exhibit for the 100th anniversary of the Triangle Factory Fire would ignite my passion for this chapter of United States history and bring me directly to the inspiring achievements of Frances Perkins. Workers' rights, women's rights, safety issues, child labor, minimum wage, Social Security: all lead to Frances, a trailblazer of exceptional courage and character. With the encouragement of the Frances Perkins Center in Newcastle, Maine, I am honored to highlight Frances' far-reaching accomplishments. Whenever the process of book-making had me stymied, I sought Frances' extraordinary resolve.

This period of history also intrigues me because my grandfather was living and working in Lower Manhattan at the time of the fire. He, like my father, worked in textiles in New York City, as did I, early in my career. Today, I love to build my collage illustrations using cut papers and photographs, as well as the laces, fabrics, and trims of the textile industry that is woven into the fabric of my family's history. I hope that my book will inspire readers to become involved when wrongs need to be righted and to see that, with steadfast determination, good can grow from tears that fall if we can find the courage to walk through open doors.

❧ SELECTED BIBLIOGRAPHY ❧

Brooks, David. *The Road to Character*. New York: Random House, 2015.

Colman, Penny. *A Woman Unafraid: The Achievements of Frances Perkins*. New York: Atheneum, 1993.

Downey, Kirstin. *The Woman Behind the New Deal*. New York: Anchor Books, a Division of Random House, Inc., 2010.

Greenwood, Barbara. *Factory Girl*. Toronto: Kids Can Press, 2007.

Keller, Emily. *Frances Perkins: First Woman Cabinet Member*. Greensboro, NC: Morgan Reynolds Publisher, 2006.

Kramer, Barbara. *Trailblazing American Women: First in their Fields*. Berkeley Heights, NJ: Enslow Publishers, 2000.

Marrin, Albert. *Flesh and Blood so Cheap: The Triangle Fire and its Legacy*. New York: Alfred Knopf, 2011.

Von Drehle, David. *Triangle: The Fire that Changed America*. New York: Atlantic Monthly Press, 2003.

Wignot, Jamila, Mark Zwonitzer, Michael Murphy, and Joel Goodman. *Triangle Fire*. United States: PBS Distribution, 2011. DVD.

www.ingramcontent.com/pod-product-compliance
Lightning Source LLC
Chambersburg PA
CBHW041323290426

44108CB00004B/115